THE MUSE SINGS

THE MUSE SINGS

DENNIS COOLEY

The Muse Sings

Design by M. C. Joudrey and Matthew Stevens.
Layout by Matthew Stevens and M. C. Joudrey.

Published by At Bay Press September 2020.

Library and Archives Canada cataloguing in publication is available upon request.

ISBN 978-1-988168-36-4

Printed and bound in Canada.

This book is printed on acid free paper that is 100% recycled ancient forest friendly (100% post-consumer recycled).

First Edition

10 9 8 7 6 5 4 3 2 1

atbaypress.com

for Mnemosyne

INTRODUCTION

The muse, we learn, or are told, or come to believe, visited in unexpected moments. She (and she was usually a she when men did the making) sparked and sustained you. The poet, at least one of romantic bent, spoke of being quickened into purpose and, if things went well, into actually doing something.

Excited, we would be brought out of ourselves; enthused, we would be possessed by the gods. In a glimmer, a word, in recall - and the mother of the muses, Mnemosyne, we remember, brought the gift of memory. Another name for inspiration, perhaps, a way to name the inexplicable - what seems given to you. Beguiled, we never forget the muse, age-old figure who purportedly has inspired poets and musicians, painters and dancers.

In *The Muse Sings* an inept supplicant woos a muse inclined to withhold her favours, to feel irked with her role, and to resent his thefts. The muse talks back - quite a lot. As the muse sings herself, she also sings to the poet, and sometimes she sings through him, when he courts her, solicits her songs.

The poet, the muse having spoken, or failed to speak, or refused to speak, sings in longing, in regret, in joy, in self-doubt; speaks in vexation, in self-ridicule; sings in curiosity, in play, in puzzlement, in hesitation. He sings in mock indignation, in wonder, in affection, in disappointment, in gratitude, wringing out the responses and the overtures.

The poems take turns talking to the poet. Sometimes they all talk at once.

OVERTURES

COLLABORATIONS

THE MUSE SPEAKS OUT

IN ALL THINGS

AND YOU, DEAR READER

envoi
(adapted from John Newlove)

from a pub
poets eventually
find their way
but you, dear
muse, they
never leave

OVERTURES

"Where art thou, Muse, that thou forget'st so long
To speak of that which gives thee all thy might?"
—William Shakespeare, *Sonnet 100*

what is your name

he said the man
with the sad brown eyes
he had touched me
where the moon bone
floats with its five satellites

said he loved her blue
green eyes had
adorned my straw
blonde hair

had grown ridiculous
ly fond of my freckles
reckless beyond belief
praised the curl of my toes
the colour of my dreams

what is your name he said
he needed to know
my name he said
he was somebody
or other he said but
he couldn't let it go
wouldn't let me go
until he knew
he had to know

who was i
anyway
& couldn't i say
a little   more

                              couldn't i   just
stay   a little longer

what is there for him in my name
and who was he to ask

            what it is
                  what is it
                        to play excited & reluctant dancer
                              answer to a perfect stranger
                  muse to a stricken man
                  blushing & sunburnt angel to everything
                              he writes

my fair lady

the lady inside
the smell of fried onions
and the glass windows
that if the small boy stood
in the light in the right spot
would send himself back

in strange and wonderful
dress she sat under
the carnival lights
the wheel that clacked red
and black the thick arm "round
and round and round it goes"
the shining hope of his dime

        learned to listen
for the high rinse in his body

he had come for the moment
when she turned, looked up,
and it ran   through him
slid over the top   and out
under years and years later
shivered in his groin

where she sat and
turned her head
looked into his eyes
passed her hands over

the snap & muffle of
cards that said
they would happen

when her left hand
reached hesitatingly
out of the booth
through the slot

dropped the
silent words
into his hand

it is a calling

she said

a calling out
a calling forth
a calling upon
a calling to
a calling up
a calling for

he said

it is a calling

she said

what this naming is
this writing then
a calling

he said

for   up   to   upon   forth   out
he was calling out her name

) she wondered if he
was trying to preposition her
& could there ever be a calling off

when she heard or thought
it was a listening to
an entering in to

they said

where they keep the ghosts
a trying to name

the dead

qu'appelle
(for Cathy Beveridge)

every day & every night
a medley of coyotes & insects
        sing *a cappella*

at dawn when sun ambushes them
in the first messy light
she flees among the dry grasses
        where deer have lain
past the clump of trembling aspen
                light / shadow /
        light /shadow

passed the sweetness of mustard & clover
flowers dusty with their modest dress
the speckles of blue & yellow

up to her ankles splashing to her shins
        to knees hips chest neck
        she is disappearing
        into a cleft in the world
        where the coyotes last night
        in sudden thrill
        had cornered something

            it is here she calls
                at first softly
        who is it please
            are you there

his voice she thinks, it is him, calling
and then a   thin-chill cry

qu' appelle

someone must have   spoken
from the back of her throat

qu'app
         elle

((elle
      (((elle

all she could think to say

who's there
        who is it

please
who is   there

the petulant poet

why this presumption   of naming she asks
the moon's inflation   its crazy dehydration

hydra or hydro it made no difference
he was the same old fool
nail bent in his brain
swollen like a squid with fantasies

he railed non-stop
rallied when her words
heady and exhilarating said
he had eyes for nothing
but her, the muse that is,
and he stuck to her keen as a beetle
in an empty beer bottle

he having met the muse

having misbehaved himself
having descended unto the dead
and faced the muse
sick with dread

now must face

the redactor

1. where were you?
2. where have you been?
3. where did you go?
4. what have you done?
5. why did you go there?
6. who were you with?
7. what was her name?
8. where did you meet her?
9. how long have you known her?
   a. how well do you know her?
   b. how long did you stay?
   c. what did she say?
   d. what was her name?
   e. when did you go?
   f. why did you go?
   g. who was she?
   h. when did she say?
   i. how did she say?
   j. who did you say?
   k. what did she have to say?
   l. what was her name?

i. why did you meet her?
ii.   what were you expecting?
iii.   why did you say that?
iv.   will you see her again?
v.   when will she be back?
vi.

      1. why did you have to go
      2. and say that?

there in the plaid light

in broad day light in plain sight
she played with his affections
pried them from his small & frightened heart

        lady lady how you toy
        with me & my tennis ball
        heart the pleas I let loose plop plop
            at your feet trying to please

      how petty it all seems how paltry
      my unshuttered heart
      you slap like a mosquito & i shudder

        when i court your affections
        you return mine archly achingly
        to the furthest corners of courtesy

        when i approach the net hoping
        for some small return
        you boom it back
        cross court in loud rejoinders
        in backhand compliments

        you serve me ill madam
      i do not deserve these passing shots

when you stand constant as Thor & as tough
at the net you have strung between us
and you keep lobbing grenades
i know i have been courting
disaster plain & simple

my heart stutters when you slam
it into an empty pail and yell
love at the top of your lungs

buried you in the grave

yard that is my heart
                    flash-frozen with grief

          your offences a heap of small-crab
          letters you never sent

i will put an end to what's left
of your refusals and recriminations
dump them face-first into the muskeg

              stuff them with thistles and ragweed
              among leaves and twiggy things
              preserve you like a Piltdown
              Man you live in ice
              & gravel or Tollund
              Man cap intact in a bog
              with your loopy grin
              stalled inside the tundra

                  can't help thinking
                  you will still be
                  suffering from frost
bite when they haul you
          /jaw intact
                        out from the peat
                        up from the permafrost
                        that is my deepfreeze heart

the internet muse strikes again

Kikki Aldridge reassuringly claims she has "waited for you."
Ashley May Katie Annastasiya Anunturi Kikki all write
missives of promised adventure. Jeany and Natie have also
waited for you. Rebecca offers "Descopera Aventura Gllotto."
He's not sure he should try to find out.

The Italians make him edgy. How do they all get through
so easily? And what if he answered? They have managed
to bypass the filters with temptations which, he is almost
thankful, he cannot understand.

The husky-voiced and wicked Russians prove even more
pressing. One greets him enthusiastically "Annastasiya
Good evening!!!" Who is this Anastasiya in whatever spelling
or address that he should listen? An enterprising "Russian-
DreamBride" posts a crisp ad: "A Beautiful Bride Could
Be Yours. Exclusive access and instructions found here."

The CAA Manitoba gets caught up in the excitement and
writes to ask "What's Your Heart's Desire?"

Miss Ann William spurns hints of romance to promise
untold wealth if only he . . . . "Good evening!" declaims Jeany
brightly. Lusy Kikki, too. Natie Ashley Cramer are also glad
to write, they remember me, they want to get acquainted.
Casi has been seeking for her true love and wonders is it
me. Another, anonymous, finds "this is sooo nervewracking."
Lusy sighs "I finally found you." What will she do now that
she has? Jeany Baldwin chummily wonders "How is it going?"

And then, more forthrightly, claims (if it is still her) that "the video" will provide "the method."

Ashley Cramer writes simply, neighbourly. What's her next move? Myong says "I wanna offer u to to go to a date with me," what did I think? Kikki Clifford is more gentle, romantic: "I hope you will like my smile." "Hey there!" writes Katie White in a note of breezy cheer.

Ashley, unperturbed, shows up again, darkly hints of a "Sexy woman." Wild Russian girls want to meet him, he should search online now. Another warmly, disarmingly he thinks, sends "Kiss to you." Ashley persists in various permutations of names and addresses.

The importunities pour in.
They all hope to hear from him soon.

the poet's letter of surcease & submission
(for Barbara Schott)

pain i can take
also disdain & reprisal
what more can a poet hope

go ahead and deliver a little grief
why spare the wrangle & bicker

the odd word of humiliation
wouldn't hurt

i can live with that
i can take that
you won't catch me by surprise
in a ganglion of hurt

have learned to prize all you can send
and to accept the scoffing

happy to praise the package of scorn
neatly wrapped in twine and barb wire

wait for it C.O.D. at the door
with pliers and a smile in my hand

postcard to
the muse

dear ▓▓▓▓▓

seeing this bed made me   & believe you
me baby think of ▓▓▓ & of me &   was and
the ▓▓▓▓ ▓▓▓ you ▓▓▓ in it i keep   was
fine & the ▓▓▓▓ were thinking of your ▓▓▓
▓▓▓▓ too & the ▓▓▓ in the of how
your ▓▓▓ would ▓▓▓ all of the ▓▓▓ was ▓▓
feel on my ▓▓▓▓ when   & so were the ▓▓
& worst ever i ▓▓▓ & of how best of all the ▓▓▓ ▓▓▓ much fun it wld be
▓▓▓ ▓▓▓ ▓▓ -- ▓▓ with you & ▓▓▓ you on the ▓▓ i wish i cld   yrs in
▓▓ ▓▓▓ you on the ▓▓ & ev-ery time i think of ▓▓▓▓ ▓▓▓ i think
of ▓▓ you & ▓▓▓▓ you all night long of you ▓▓ my ▓▓▓ our ▓▓ of
i wish you wld ▓▓ me & tell me you want to ▓▓ me & that you too were
dreaming of ▓▓▓ me & ▓▓▓▓ me to. ▓▓▓ with you

he writes to the muse

Respectfully yours, Yours sincerely, Respectfully, Yours truly,
Sincerely, Sincerely yours, Yours faithfully, Appreciatively,
Kind regards, Thank you, Regards, Best regards, Salutations,
Godspeed

Cordially, Cordially yours, Gratefully, Godspeed, Thank you,
Many thanks, Thanks, Best wishes, All best, Yours, Good
wishes, Once again, Admiringly, Your friend, Wishing you
well, Best wishes for your future, Hoping to hear from you,
I look forward to hearing from you,

Warmest personal regards, For now, Until next time, Till
tomorrow, Fondly, Happily, Warmly, Take care, Much love,
Love, With love,

Missing you, Missing you always, Please remember me, All
my love, Much happiness, With all my love, With all my
heart, With all of my love, Now and forever, Ever yours, All
my love, Forever yours, Now and ever,

Soon, Always and forever, Eternally yours, Ever yours, Ever
and Always, Never ending, Always yours, Always, Yours,

xoxoxoxoxoxoxox,

Impatiently, I'll be in touch, Can't wait, Lots of Love,
Expectantly, Can't wait until you are back, Till the day
I see you again,

Later, Cheers, Adios, So long, Keep it real, See you later,
Be good, Love and kisses, Loaves and fishes, Onward and
upward, Can't wait, Hugs and kisses, Hear from you soon,
Talk to you later, Be seein' ya,

I remain, Lady, Your Most Humble and Obedient Servant,
May I live always to serve you and your crown,

Until we meet again,

when will i ever see you again
my god i miss you

why don't you fucking write

                        please write

touché

s\he touched herhim some where on the shoulder
(they had been out of touch) and put himher to the touch
they were calling it close even though they feared
it might touch off a falling out shee was no easy touch
no simple push-over (look but don't touch)

       hshe wondered if s|he herhim self
       as such would prove to be a touch off
       sooner or later they might touch a nerve a sore spot
       one or both of them touched by what was said
       & felt even though they had almost lost
       touch with reality and oneanother
       a sense of touch they both swore

hes|he never touched the stuff   /never
but when shess reached to touch
swore heesh had the touch the royal touch
and could touch up the worst moments
it was the right touch they agreed

       whatever it was touched off the words
       nothing could touch them yet
       they brought a touch of blood
       to their cheeks shee touched heimr off
       ever since someone had put them in touch
       no one could touch hiherm

    it was then it touched home
    it touched on big issues they thought, delicate matters
    nothing touched hehirm nothing phased hierm

the way shhe touched hierm up for a while
and the times hhes touched him deeply

it was well worth it just being touched by rhe somehow
eh thought esh should touch up ish manners and said
touching on such matters felt hshe had it coming

          & all the time was thinking
          hse was a bit touched and rather
          touchy though hee himself was
          out of touch, true, and things were
          way over shi head

heshe felt a touch of fever found hihemsrelf wishing
for just a touch more s/he had the right touch
she had a touch for things
when she applied the finishing touches

she could see he really was touched
          and he carried a torch
        for her touch in truth he had been
pleasingly teasingly touched had grown
attached to her touch it had been touch
& go for a while he had been hoping
they would keep in touch no matter
what s/he would never lose the touch

                it was then he knew
it had been a touching moment
              he had been well
          and truly touched

clippety clop

supposing i really were
a hoop
and by grace fallen
off the wheel what if
i were to up & fly
(off the barrel   / off the handle:
off the wagon would get
yr attention)

in clear sight of you & headed west
clippety clop clippety clop
where you revel
in your fixed and rigid course
where though you reveal nothing
under the singe of wind and the siege of sun
you sing your head off
so long it's bin good
and you rumble haughtily past all water
holes breathing dust & hollering
i bin every there man
cross the burning land man

does this solve anything
or absolve you   /really
this loud & unseemly whooping
this clinging to the north
star this terrible ab
using of my affections abs
conding with all my caring

you with alarm watching
me veer off into a slough
and thoughts of you
middle of my brain
stuck in the mud
without a rim
on the edge
of the hor
izon
!

you in sudden surprise crying out
what a great time to leave me loose wheel

broken hearted

you've finally gone
              & done it
                , well,
you had to–didn't you–jam the dear
john billets doux, adieu, every
one of them into his red
and blue postal
-box special deli
very chique heart
with a lid that swung
hopefully open

had to drop off the heart
ache in confused metaphors
and talk of billy too

smashed up his heart as if
it were a christmas bulb
or a discarded mickey of rye
you could stomp underfoot
in which dozens of crickets had perished
singing their hearts out

of course there will be
an in quest no quest
ion of that even if
the papers you know will say
though slight your affections
you were the light of his life

velodrome

just before she left
she revved and burbled
in a round black smoke

talk of her departure
made him cough
his eyes smart

her noisy rapture churned inside
his heart lined with SAE-40
a terrible viscosity and she
circled the velodrome that was
his skull at a terrible velocity

the electricity compressed to an electron
snapped in blue sparks
in greater & greater brightness
singed his eyebrows
the hairs in his nostrils

empress of centrifuge she revolved
furiously against all gravity
a ferocity that knew no compass

and then
Bburrbbb **Bbburrrb** *Brbrrr* *Ubb*-Ubb
/she was gone

whirled into distant orbits
a small dot in a sky full of sprinkly things
nothing but wobbles and loops and ellipses

      and he was left
nothing but a sad and small obit
                rubbing his eyes
                   his blood
           breaking down
starting to ping and smoke

a trick with a truck

                            it is
        a backing
                            \ \ up

        your heart skids in on
                empty and on
                            a ruffle of air
                            a tickle of hair

            the box rising
        high at first
            a small trickle
                & then a
        gravel sigh & **whu-ump**//
        it bumps /
                // it is empty

            JUST LIKE THAT
                            you are dumping me
                            and i am watching you
                            back-firing as you go

            truck box bouncing
            on country music full bore
            banging away in a pillar of dust
    till i am beginning to feel more
    than a little like landfill
    an anthill that's been run over

never fail you failing
            to signal when
)the thrill of that- you
hit the road, hair whipping in the wind

            & no one can see you for dust

courting

she bounces on the balls
of her feet leaps
she leaves her feet
she slashes the air
he in tentative overtures speaks
sometimes returns   )achingly
back to the back of courtesy

mostly when he takes the words
out of the cart and imagines
some small return
none of her bone-crushing
base-line backhanded blows
the grunts that hammer them back
a terrible racket when she smashes
every one of them cross
court in loud & curt replies

his best attempts weak, out of bounds,
into the net, crushingly returned,
nothing but skids and slices

it is his heart she tosses above her head
threatens with one whap to
burst like a blood-laden mosquito
splatter worse than a tomato

tightly strung in her sun
-dried heart she stands
at the net she has fastened
between herself and his upstream hurt

there you have it

the moment a
cork bonked into a bottle

and there it was
there you were
would you were
there i mean
i mean there would be good
if only you were there

here i mean
i mean here is where
you should be
if you would be any where

there there yd say
where are we yd say
& id say here
right here
here is where it's at

& you wld say
well maybe not
may be it's neither
here nor there

there it is then
isn't it
& there it'd be
there i'd be

left wondering here
about there
& where there would be
if you yanked the t out
like a bad tooth
or a bent nail

here we are now then
there we would be
there we'd have it
and where would we be

mnemonics

preserved in the blog you have kept
and accusingly laid at my feet

the melody no remedy
for an old malady dwelling on
                    old grievances
the day—perverse, persevering

                    until you pop
                    in bulging foglights
                    and old grievances

preserved in your boggy past
a membrane against memory

                    i wld be im
                    per: me able my
                    self but there it is
                    it's all yours
                    your doing

                    it's all over now
                    all over your face
                    it is your face
                    collapsing to the one
                    you left behind

unh   uhnn

                                        she said
                        pulling alongside
a story in tow and
                            she hastened into the street

they were freighted with meaning, her words
he was frightened of what she might say
could there be any pleasing of the muse
or appeasing of disdain

            he couldn't understand
                            the moist & huffy sounds
her thoughts hoisted onto the air
            in a luminous halo

                        no no it's no bother
                        not really she said
                            she liked it

                        she did it
                        all the time

            her exhalations shone
                    where she looped them
                        alive as northern lights

sometimes when it was winter
                    and her face red with cold
                        she would pull her breath
            in gray mittens over his face

COLLABORATIONS

"And this is true. For the poet is a light and winged and holy thing, and there is no invention in him until he has been inspired and is out of his senses, and the mind is no longer in him"
— Plato, *Ion*

they come down with a bad case of poetry

i cannot scan nor ken
what lines your mind
grown so faint it could have been
scratched by birds on sandstone
or drawn with a stick in the heart

no wonder she said you cannot
the sky is humming with molecules
the aspirations of chloroform
the hammering of spiders

the whole creation's become
nothing for you but leftovers
from a castiron pan

as for me (meaning me, poet or her,
self, muse) what is to
become of the light
markings on the skin

the little pile of memories
moraines left from the ice-age
migraines in the mind of god

our thoughts small pebbles
in a passing glacier

they make beautiful music

i learned to breathe properly, a fat deep breathing i could
feel everywhere, no fooling all the way through, upon the
currents. it is to draw, oxygen in halation to the brain the
bright, bubble and flare of cells, the scatter and blur the
danger of, never learning how to blow, air through the
instrument train the, embouchure to the mouthpiece across
in, love of which the musician blows and we, make beautiful,
music hear at night the darkness lapping, softly as it is
passing over, the waters what in love we yearn for, learn,
proper breathing, in air prosper, the grace of prospero, fair
of face, the monday muse, the music, blessed, you treat with
care, warm it slowly, to ease of tongue, shape of mouth and
lips, shipshape, smooth in practice, the comfort of lips and
reed, a feel for, the soft touch, the little breathy whoops and
coughs all the farty sounds of water every last warty bump

and so it came about that she greeted me with parted lips,
we met lip to lip, we an ellipsis in oh, a trip on two lips to
heaven, the fingers moving freely, having a touch for it, the
rhythmic breath, pattern of the piece. discovered i could
create everything using just breath and fingers a skilled and
delicate fingering music from our warm bodies it was swing
and sway we embraced through and through we weren't sure
we could get away, with it we got into, trouble when i tried
tapping, my foot it was there, that she put her foot, down
and i missed, a step i lost my place the palace of, our playing
our rhythm the cheek of that woman she didn't turn a hair
though she turned my head, and didn't i know what it was to
be up and down the scales the stairs didn't i say it was a hair's

breadth escape when she let \ her breath out it made the hair
stand on my neck i was so embarrassed i had put my foot in
i was trying to get my feet under our waltz under way the
two-step too but she, goody two-shoes, grew wary, stepped
on my good times,

stomped's the word,

he *(almost)* **escapes with the muse**

the plane sputters and coughs
thumps thumps down the runway
it gasps and lurches slightly to the side
shivers in clutter and consternation

      a gaggle of people
      running clumsily
as if they were loose luggage
in tow or fallen off the cart
and a lot of angry poets in a flap
rags on the tail of a kite

the poet and the muse
have commandeered a plane
and they are taxiing for take off
runaways on the tarmac

come back you son of a bitch
where the hell do you think you're going
they flail and shout, stumble, shake their fists
a mob closing on Quasimodo

the poet hunches over the throttle
launches himself against their gravity
begs and calls down affliction
upon the weight of the world
the muse puts her left hand on his right shoulder
anxious they will never get off the ground

the plane shakes and tremours
sags into a terrible fit of coughing
the ragged pursuit rallies
their spirits lift, they are closing fast
all of them cursing and lurching
swept in their own flyting
the poets worst of all

the plane splutters and begins to
          slouch into itself
          hiccoughs and dies

you selfish bastard they holler what the hell
are you doing with the muse
you can't have her all to yourself
she's our muse too you know

first edition

the landscape scraped by ice
in acts of sedition the letters
snapped like gravestones

rocks in greetings left behind
form splotches on the face of the earth
watermarks my dad found
and in rocks compiled

words i entered faith
fully blue & yellow
scribblers page after page
leaving muddy prints

you, muse, want me to learn
clarity /the rarity of
a new script in a small neat hand
                digital, you say

poke holes in what i write
insert prickly messages
bloodred emendations

insist upon your
edicts for the ice age

poetry: the ins and outs of

have added glowing rubrics
and placed in the margins
small and exquisite notes
a red letter day

in strange languages
something shows through
to put a shine on

> who'd have thought
> would be our undoing
> houdini inside the lines
> drawn in ropes and chains
> incandescent with moving

> would surely have listened
> and spoken with the dead

dearly departed
(after Robert Kroetsch)

it is the same old question
the four women hurtle into particles
and in elements disport

1. she of air
2. she of water
3. she of earth
4. she of fire

four who are for ever preceding
who draw themselves beyond calling

all your life they said
is a search for the dead

always the woman
on verge of speech missed
in a gust of departure gone

an impossible search for the lost
Daphnes who flee light
-footed fleet-footed Persephones
oh knee oh arm oh face
who drop into darkness
among the potatoes and turnips

in every story the woman vanishes
in his broken letters crosses
the stringy pastures of his vigil
over brome and fescue
beyond reach or rescue

a dream enfolding memory
the warm hands of the mother

who is most there
pressing upon the silence

his musings
(for Douglas Reimer)

they have climbed aboard his sleep
long-limbed dreams reimer
has taken in and now is keeper of
believer in if, listener of yes

he anxiously pours milk into a saucer
has clicked open one after another
little tins of sardines, hazelnuts, sun
flower and sesame seeds
set them out in the hall

he has strained to hear the iron
lung coughing in the basement
the small crack under the door sucking
his breath like a lemon cough-candy
listens to the voices in the laundry room
that chew like carpenter ants on his thoughts
that rattle in the vents rumble the ducts to his heart
all night they stumble down pipes in the walls
the scratchings of the quick & the dark

reimer looks for the writing in the kitchen sink
searches the bathroom tiles the cellar door
reimer cannot choose cannot close
his ears nor his heart to the yowls and nibbles

reimer lies in wide-awake astonishment
knows there are lesions in the stars lessons to be sought
he is eager for night fearful he will miss the signs
if only he had word enough and rhyme
all night long reimer talks with the visitants
which arrive like pills he spills, or beans,
his heart a shaken and fizzy bottle
he lifts from a cruet

a flamboyant and a foolish thing, fishing
for flies in the soya-sauce night, he flings
his lines hand over hand over hand
until his breath plunks with a sigh into the darkness
                    until it goes slippery and
            quick he tries to reel it back

                        when he hits a rough patch he
                        lifts his arm like a referee
                            about to call a penalty
                        lone as an umpire
                                at home about to call
                        the game because of darkness

        listen he says listen
        and if you really do
        if you really listen
                    you can

                            hear the wind
                    in his heart

chiasmus

cross words we play at cross purposes
our words cross-hatched
in division or alignment also
in singing love signing love
letters a question of what is excised
and brought to nought
what in wonder thought or said in joy
Xs & Os & tic-tac-toe it keeps us
on our toes, our fingers crossed

untold names and unsaid places
X marks the plot what yet is to be
terra in cognita X names unexplored regions
and unknown parts we're headed for

we come across what lies between us
what's gone amiss or missing
and unaccounted for what is plain
wrong or incorrect at certain
times it means greek design

XOXOXOXOXOXOXOXOXXOXOXOX

it shows your hand at the end of the day
at the end of the letter
it announces star-crossed lovers
in chance encounters & games of dice
a strike which if twice repeated means you're out
means figures lost in overlapping,
a chiasmus, a crossing of paths,

a chasm in denial or contradiction

it never crossed my mind
zoons she cried, ma
dame X, it's e'en eek
regret zed all over again in the end an X
-it is one big fat zero the sacred X
a matter of faith & suffering
Ixion for his illicit love fixed to a fiery cross

      which is why it is X
      -rated the show for
      bidden pleasures hidden treasures
      exposed only in fitting
      measures a little flushed
      in leisure hush-hush my love my
      sterious you your serious X
      an instance of assent an affi
      xing of name to contract a making contact

strange & powerful surging in X
    ray fashion the tremble
      in an unknown power
      if $x + x = 2$ unknowns
          if they come across
the letter chi as in chiasmus
      subject to last-minute can
      cellations to things X-ed out
      in double cross lost & long forgotten
      blood in correction streaming
      like ink down the page

the poet loves her machines

(for Nicole Markotić)

loves the way
the printer
clicks in dismay or in pleasure moves
its arm
seeks permission

stirs at   the end
lifts   slightly
excitement excitement

the printer sleeps
for hours on the desk
a silent promise
a premise of   love she loves
the small spasms of discovery
or pleasure
when it sighs

ahhh the printer says
she has heard
what the computer has thought
and hoped against loneliness to say
thrilled to its unruffled talk

she waits for
the moments when
it quickens and she can hear
the husky music of its breathing

"would you believe"
(after Maria Wisława Anna Szymborska)

*

would you believe
every night i turn into cleo
patra veritable tornado of passion rid
iculous inside   the thickets of night
not though i sicken   with desire
i wouldn't swap it   for anything

i peep i cheep   like a sparrow
the seeds of patrician love
in four-part harm
ony only thing is

the long-haired dog i lead
loves me rubs himself
against me offers
muzzle & snuff

he loves me loves me more
than all the words in all the world

*

i can't complain   all my lovers are pliant
and fleshy-lobed   most of the time
firm as bamboo when i ask   or ever i wish

would you believe when it comes down to it
i lay them smack on the kisser

big wet warm ones and i moan
the way i imagine she did or must have

all night i crawl on darkness
and beside me with enviable ease
                    an eel glides
rainy words blowing from its side
the room billowing with pearl-grey silk

the guy at the easel is
oozing carmine & aqua marine &
if you don't mind my saying so
i brighten when he touches
shiver when he daubs the paint and it
slides in fresh water over

                              *

              i am perfectly able
        to disown all the nos and nots and nevers
        thank you   it's a snap setting aside
        the no times and no wheres and no bodies
        the inestimable craving for cravats

        it's the busy bodies cause the real stink
        it's itch of sweater   wince of fly
        within an inch of your life

          *

but listen just the other day   i saw
twins in plaid tights   plummet
two suns   unwinding into the flax

and walk away clean as new linen
Legacy Collection Deco from Harrods
        happy   as foxes singing
                    love is a many
        -splendoured thing
all rosewater and laughter

                    *

        tomorrow night i expect   to meet casa
        nova at the Apple computer store   he will be
        wide-eyed where he   will yank
        open a paisley   curtain and hold
                                the door

        as if i were   entering
        a castle or   movie theatre
        or (best of all   wish be blest) a
        hushed &   velvet boudoir

        looks for all   the world insouciant
        and his hand   trembling slightly
        with adoration clear   as anything
        sure as i am   standing here
        when in chivalry   he winks
        and says *come on in   why don't i*
            mi casa   es su casa

What am I waiting for?

the prairie muse explains her role :
(for Dick Harrison)

Yes, she says, first you call his name. He likes that, it perks him up. He's been squeaking by the screen door, preening with sun and all the hurtin' songs he can remember.

Everyone can see it happening.

Her voice comes in a beautiful long loop, an elegant ballet, and he, roused, ducks, **plop**. She watches the little puff of dust.

She has been a little pokey but she knows what she is doing. She knows the trajectory of love. She knows the shorts are too slow and he longs for something more. She does too. She knows what he will do. He can hear her coming, he has an ear for those things. She needs to send him a bullet deux, a quick reply, a loud retort. One that will get him where he lives.

She has already squeezed, already let go the second one. She sends it in the hot and crinkly air, music to his ear. She hears it mew as it goes. He has heard her calling, he cannot resist, cannot say no. He is pleased pleased beyond all holes he could ever dig, all the dust & sun he could ever doze in. She has loosened her voice and he has heard the high zing in his already heart. Up he pops, he can't wait. He wants an earful of

love. And—**PLUP**—she plugs him. Drops him on the lip of dirt—

bang—loud and ringing in his ear.

                              a spent cartridge at her feet

Dear Dubé,
(for Paulette Dubé)

though i grow doubtful
whether Our Lady
of Perpetual Help Pool Hall
still saves from miscues
or rescues any one
           i want to be there
i want to be without hesitation
           lifted from inertia
a pool ball white as a leper
interloper, in collusion among

the red & rolling hearts want to
carom among the blue and brown and green
see the black and pink and yellow ones
perpetually rolling and shining

there where they brush
against the cushions
nudge other hearts
that click happily in collision

i want to be a part of the thousand
shocks flesh is err to
that pool of help & forgiveness

exactly when, their lines true, they clear the table
with all the joy & clatter they can muster

Les Habitués des Billiards
as once they wrapped the dead
Mary, Queen of Scots,
in felt from her billiard table
a final game of billets-doux

& you cool pool hall poet
when they chalk one up
you ain't even flustered

                                                      ? are you
        indubitably you
                              oh Dubé
            oh do be do be do

my great wish she said
(for Lea Graham)

i.

to feel the words humming
at my ear backwards, upside
down, mid-air the long tongue

remembered the carmine & canary yellow
dreamt vermillion & coppergreen
flameblue & magenta the iridescent birds
that sped high in the Andes
bright as crayons
their hearts beating fast

ii.

thought also of Linseed oil Larch Turpentine Dammar Crystals,
Mastic Colophony Carnauba Wax Copal

knew they would be encaustic the caramels & honeys & resins
the long smooth loops of colour
shining like the man who flew
into the wax that was
as if the heat were true & pure

be careful to draw the pigment from the camel hair brush
with the surface which may be warm for rivering
the tinted paste if cool the brush
stroke will freeze immediately

iii.
in the end if you are
lucky there is a burning
during which heat is passed over
a fusing & a bonding
if desired there then can be

a polishing with a soft cloth
a nice sheen a warm glowing
the light from the yellow
wax could be a sun
flower leaning toward

best results can be achieved
with practice and for those
who are willing to trust
their hearts and see what works

iv.
listen to see if she were singing
sweeter than calypso into his ear

the holy font

the marks are skinny with want have grown
shiny threads monks hope plainly to wear
in time to mend their ways
attend to widows & orphans
reach those in distress

wld teach you   to touch   touché   to each yea even
unto thy toenails i myself
reach for the patches on your mistakes
where they glow like parables

in no time you will inspect the faces
for sin and error, crook and blemish,
you will count all the arms & beaks every
counter & loop even unto bars stems balls through thick
strokes and thin strokes thin folks and much too thick
folks themselves become ascenders & descenders
on base lines & mean lines all the weights & widths

& every bowl a heart, void, you hold
in pincers study the face beard neck scrutinize
shoulder belly body shank stem nick
mull over every groove & foot
no mean fete the meticulous detail
you disclose to the printer's devil
knowing there will be hell to pay

you inspect the ~~frames~~ flames with inquisitional zeal
all this do you ponder in your leaden heart
minutely measure the dart of flies, the dirt in hairline fractures
the page you mail the world dotted with flyspecks
over the love you in long script write
the many colours you hang in the burning window

the 12th letter

he has heard her
turning storms with her feet

s\he wishes s/he heard
s\he thinks s/he remembers

wonders if s\he will
recall and speak

the Greek alphabet
the 12th letter

the 12th of ever
the 12th disciple

before the baker's dozen
makes you think

it holds them
in shaky suspension

when it strings
across the hot tin

sky μ heshe thinks
shhe thinks of μ

he wonders if
she will think of him

wherein they dispute

so what if i have
mixed the metaphors
who cares if i come

like iambs to the laughter what of it
what of those who made light
wondering of and went their ways

one to the farm an
other to his merchandise
would you hear my lungs coughing
like bread rising
beyond notice my heart
smoking faintly like a ham

holy smokes you will say
the quick flame in your face
wondering if you yourself will
crank it up to hurricane

what if you were
to say is that *right* is **that**
right and just
supposing you or i or
both and no holding back
no bother
took a deep breath

watched for the moment
the light has swollen
to a gassy sigh of yeast

shiny as a toenail
big as a tonsil
way larger than a goitre

earrotics
(for Charlene Diehl)

a whirring and whaling
so loud it tickles her
pink she wants to play it
by ear, she has a good
ear, to ear is human

in a tight spot somewhere between
cochlea & vestibule living on burrowed
time she says it comes & goes,
rumbles like a rock, rhotic,
on an ice flow carries
messages when she moves
falls out in clatters
like pebbles it scratches
& deposits at her feet
a penguin in seek- and bless- ing

winter drops rocks
brought on glacial sleds
broken loose from the arctic
erratics in the inner ear
the warm canals & channels

she listens for
it *ticks ticks ticks*
quite the earful something

close as waiting,
a message from the other
side of blood
whispering in italic

arias she remembers as a
fulvous aching in the ear

badly muddled

                  the whole garden   shot

FOR IN HER LOOK SHE WITHERETH
BUSHES SPLITTETH ROCKS & BY THE EYE

           (the fossil eyes)

SPITTETH POISON FORTH

       every radish and every carrot frozen solid
       the tomatoes grown desultory and drooping

           in the dead grass & cat tails
         all alone   & so forth

   a frog huddled
        in the ditch
                little boy blue
  is turning to mud

        the sudden cold
        & the giving of the Eve
        Ill Eye

X

Xerxes at the hot portal, Thermopylae defined,
Greeks by the cleft gate at Delphi,
what speaks and stirs,

when they ask for the X
an asterisk in the heavens
or John Donne "A bracelet
of bright hair about the bone"
if we in the nexus of our affections
should enter chasm, isthmus, peninsula, delta

our paths were bound to cross in an X a schism our guarded
selves to the other side into shadows the shades of Hades
we waded a darkness that slid into our eyes the warmth
going out our days mixed at the railway to our selves the
cross-winds blowing the boundaries where Hemingway
drove the Red Cross ambulance saw chi at the shrines on
the rural roads in Germany Christ lying forever in his
mother's arms and the cars plunging through the
Kreuzweg

Pompeii

(i.)

A brown-eyed woman,
green tunic, purple mantle,
studies something we cannot see.
She wears a gold-rimmed hat, gold earrings. A
stylus in her right hand. She touches it, the tip,
to her lips, which are lightly closed. Four
wooden tablets, bound, in her left hand (she
has just read? inscribed? is waiting to write?) tilted
toward her. Small punctures in the wax, letters
he hopes to carry away and read.
Words of honey and light,
Swift might have said.

(ii.)

X marks the error frequent in French still more in Greek a
lot of crossing out and red ink. Would we in our carnival-
glass lives cross over to the other side? A little jubilation? X
to see, O to see, ecstasy, to rejoice in, the air, oh!, of our ways.
jubilation jubilation jubilation air sun rain days to be em-
braced in excess, rapture. in X-celsis 100° Fahren heit, 37.8°
Celsi us

(iii.)

the molecules boiling in our hour-glass lives come between,
uncovered. we come across what lies there. the gap that is,
palpable, spanning across. agapé. time of earthquake, tremour.
Mount Etna and Vesuvius shrouded in ash the world ending
and dust poured into sudden blackness a room sealed against
light where others may discover what it is to be frozen in
flames

Nefertiti

when the land gives up its thirst
a sculptor is forced to abandon his shop
an apostle is reduced to eating
         locusts & thistle

when a head is pulled
out of the desert sand
"the beautiful one has come forth"

"You cannot describe it
with words. You must see it."
you will know what it is
to have given yourself up
and to have spoken with the dead

stylus on waxed tablet or papyrus on the Nile
and now in small script your own hand
on creased and sometimes crumpled paper

lift your head to listen
where in Berlin she rests
new with memory

if this is isis

what then this is
a missive a
near miss if
the ice is
not yet off the lake

it would be nice if
she were here but
where is isis
the crisis of that

what if isis
is all we got
if isis is here

o sir it is
her and he
her her o
she his her

o sir is
it you
back at last
in bits & pieces
together again

this is nice is
it not it
surely is is
              n't it
i mean be
ing part of an ice
age all there is

all this is
that is it

embodied

"out of Erebus came swarming up shades of the dead"
—Homer, Odyssey

           a rustle of wings, the rubber
           pigeons arrive on a gust
           a cool vapour
           as if fearing, or hoping,
           we will swap lives

seeks the thick clotted world
the soft mass of lungs
a tightening in the larynx
the wad of ligament & gristle
the horseshoe of teeth
high vault of mouth

valves   lips   teeth bared
head thrown back
throat gulps and drags
heavings in chest

also and necessarily a tongue
opening & closing
knows no guile or guise
it cries   whisks. tries to whisper

the aspirates of beginning
again what once was

dips   into the trough
          wets its   breath
its mouth   warms
          ready to   speak
the small   pops & hisses

          speaks of every
          one & every
                    thing

world of reference
(for David Arnason)

*"Electronic computation is as derivative of print as print
is derivative of script and script of sound and sound in
its turn of breathing."*—McArthur, *World of Reference*

the long nerves sprawl across the table
the computer ticks & gasps
the printer takes a deep breath
oblivious to all discretion
watches for direction

releases itself with
the urgency of confession
each page with a sigh

yes no yes no yes no yes
IOIOIO IOIOIO IOIOIO IOIOIO
the scanner jerks & talks to itself
isisosirisisisosirisisisosiris
sings to love & discombobulation

traffics in prohibition & desire
moves in scheme & impulse
in small groans & ticks

the long path our words follow
through swinging gates
we are paging one another

THE MUSE SPEAKS OUT

"By god, quod he, for pleynly, at a word,
Thy drasty rymyng is nat worth a toord!
Thou doost noght elles but despendest tyme.
Sire, at o word, thou shalt no lenger ryme."
—Geoffrey Chaucer. "The Canterbury Tales."

the muse, her powers

she slipped from night
a hempen bag
into the morning ran

sacked with the first messy light
it was time she said
time to up and go

knowing the sun
would strike

at the last
moment she would
untie and pull the thunder out
skip nimbly to the side
and seize it

by the neck feel
its thrashing
in her mouth
its life shaking
up and down
her body

why not

snap to it she said
if it was up to her
she was up to making am
ends amen to that i thought
all men shall be tailors

i knew id be all in
if it came to that ours would
be a life of knotty ties
traders on the high seas

by the end she'd have me
in stiches st itches that's me
           within inches of
a life decked out in yard goods

           as for her part she said
           she was tired of being
           admired from afar
           it was high time for an affair
           as far as she was

concerned she had had it
mired in a miasmal life

in case i hadn't noticed
in rhyme & rhythm true
making up she confided
actually hinted she was mocking
time (or stalking me
(i cldn't tell

                    was it true
              did i not agree it was
        more than meets the eye
        more than passeth under
        standing when all is sad & dun
        all the blows of mischance
        and every miserable act of miscreants
                    still plenty of time
                    to make ends meet

on the other and

why don't you then
                              take me
by the and i say
dear lady let us go
by & by let us go
                you & i
           tout de suite
in the suite buy & buy

man and woman strolling
a long the same old am
per: sand & per: say in im per
                so nation go
walking and in and and let us
take the music by the and
our ways and our
saddened days addend
thus end in id and i
dentity why don't we
go walking on the and

believe me my leman
the sun truly is a lemonade moon
in a briny marinade
and we unprimly in a prom
enade a rueful wind teasing
your hair your eyes shining
you the finest thing in all the and

in the sweet bye & bye
going to beat the and
till the and of time

of all the luck

talk about luck s/he lucked in
when s/he said s/he liked it
still i shouldn't press my luck
    when s/he looked off

into the distance and the ducks said
Luck Luck Luck in sad voices and said
s\he lacked nothing s/he didn't
know when s/he was licked
no s/he didn't yes s/he did s/he said
s,he was tickled, s,he was ok,
and things were looking good
as luck would have it

        s/he did know
        just his luck
        where and
        when s/he was
        licked that is
        s/he had been long on
        the lookout for this
        it looked bad
        long had s/he looked
        oft had s/he lacked
        the very thing
        that made her mad
        with vernal winds
        something to spring
        a leak in a pad
        locked and venal heart

aLacK aLas

said the thin-necked geese & again **aLas aLas**
a lass a lad a lack oh woe
the best laid plans & he
down on his luck down on
his knees as things turned out
she feeling down about it & now what

luck s/he couldn't believe hisher lies
keep it up s/he said and see
where it gets you

from herhis eyes tears leaked
pLock pLock into the dust
copiously conspicuously concupi
sciently pro miss
cuously silent thusly and visco
us with love talk about luck
promises promises

s/he felt s?he had a lock on love
pock pock pock the hens said
inspecting the dust pecking
the very pebbles they picked
were coming up prim
roses were looking up
it looked like rain
as luck would have it
all s/he had to do was
follow the noise feelingly

and he his nose promisingly
if it came to that
s/he could make do
s\he would take

> a licking s/he would
> > tuck him in
> to great good fortune
> of all the luck s\he could
> > take him in
> she would take a chance
> on him s\he couldn't believe
> his luck it was just
> plain dumb luck

the romantic poet delivers

a curse upon
now you have completed your course in parsimony
your heart has snapped shut in a purple purse
a blighted persimmon on a string
a shrivelled pomegranate

everyone can see you
more than fulfill your purpose
tie me up in nots and nevers

whichever way i look you are nowhere
to be found as i see it it looks

bad seeing you fading
away in a dusting of wince and grimace

you might let your light so shine
you could be a blinding lighthouse to
the rowing through the night

when the day is chill
and the darkness has come upon us

night an ink

well we fall into
and our thoughts darken

when we rise
drip onto the paper

we scan for a sign
that says we were there
            you are
                        here

that when next you arrive
we might know and find you
wherever you are
wherever you have gone

we might know
                        it is you
dog-earring the page
the marker thick with ink
and your finger prints
in a dashingly unreadable hand

LP

that's right she says
        there she is and she
's got a point
                                has the pen
                in her hand
    / right here
                            \like this
look at this she says

                and it drops
                            she drops it
    gently
        down
                        to the
            surface
                        drops it like a pin into the carbon
            paper night
                        it drifts over
                            the dark and spinning world

    how can she be sure when
        it speaks in pops and hisses
                                and lifts
                                into her mind
                        a darkblue river
                over mud and gravel

the night revolves until day scratches
                     ta–tsschkk   teh–ttkssk   teh–tkkss
                  a white noise around her
                         spins like a headache
                               like a kiss

an itch an ache

(for barry nichol)

i.

        who in such straits can argue
                what it is
        to be set along side
        a whisper a rustle

heavy with aspiration with heaving
into heaven and behaving badly

        when with a sigh she whacks
           the stubby night
    thwack thwak
        elbows it from its thick green sleep
        and with a hitch in her gait
        hauls it over the coals and the lumpy waters

ii.

        hwat s/he said
            what on earth
                or upon the waters
                    were you thinking

iii.

        oh hwere or hwair have you been
        my patchy old man how long
        you have been a scratchy aitch
        and since hwen fallen silent

iv.

hwen hwhen hwhenn you smile for me

ah **ha** the heart felt a burble the queen of hearts

pairing with others

c, g, p, s, t, w

the life and times of
what otherwise lies beside
the eighth one

v.

oh oh

here is an ᑒ

here's hoping

let us open it & see
hours are not to reason
why however it has lost
its voice taken hostage
and we no longer
have the ᑒ
to carry on

when in silence it suffers
the heart stutters
realizes hwat it means hwen
the hearth gives up on the ᑒ

vi.

       when we speak the words
          in thread or threat
         the world goes barren
       the heart torn from earth

            bereft of all **h**
              you and i
           wondering how
            it came to this
             how in **h**
            we got here

muse of a promising

nature you said it would be
a real outing this time you said
with any luck it would be
so full of advent yr sure in any event
duality we would be at least
                    reeling with joy

yes, that, and rolling you said
without a word of a lie
your eyes we were in for it
and you didn't mind
one crazy ride after another

didn't i know what is what and what
on earth was the matter with me
did i think i could resist
every last contraption of romance

you said we were you were i was
bound to misadventure at sea
so extravagant not even Lloyds would underwrite

                                    i could quit
                    a life of doubt & debenture
enough of marginal and clerical

scatter the words
any old time i wanted
right then & there
left
right
& centre

never having to justify
my lines for any one

he wldnt breathe

a word the prospect as he came upon it
was truly sublime the view so inviting
the world could hold no more happiness

and he thought then to enter that joy
such as might move & give rise to
the most intense feeling it was
one might say a brush with divinity

you got a lot of nerve mister
me who has invited you in shown you
the word in the burning bush
the shores of the promised land
the way to kingdom come

hey, i hardly got a peep
if you want to know it was
no more than a glancing blow

i stuck my neck out for you
way out, non-stop,
i was in way over my head
felt like an over-filled gerry can
guy'd get dizzy just breathing

i didn't hear a thing about how i suffered
flapped though i did like a weathercock
but no as far as you were concerned
i could yowl like the seven winds

day in and day out until i felt
like the bellows at a crematorium
and not a flicker out of you

i was a scuba diver for you i went
to the bottom of the sea
plunging for pearls
& me, i was happy, coming up
snorkeling, my ears popping

                              oh, come on

sometimes i get sea sick churning
like a paddlewheel up the mississippi
it's picked up a stiff tail wind
a high strong wind a bluster
a flurry of not knowing
why you would fritter it all away

                              come off it

when i up and come back
i will be a blues player a
beached whale raised from the dead
sea wheezing in my ears
sighing for air

                              get over it

you will weep & you will shake
a harpoon in the sky & cry
like a sharp-eyed harpy
for all you gone and done
all you so insensately tossed away

her greatest disappointments

she has seen a lot
of sighing a lot of hand
-holding and moaning and
she is sick & tired of it

let the poet get himself another muse
if he can which she very much doubts

she has passed him vowels that are soft & warm in the palm
consonants that rattle like walnuts inside his skull

what is in it for her
what was the word coming to

without pause or forethought she had
answered his sad-eyed pleas
just a few words for him

she no longer was going to bring
secret and shining songs
torn from the thickest
chambers of her fibrillating heart

he would only stuff his pockets
carry them off every morning
claiming they were his and dump them
onto the table where he would move
the pieces as if in scrabble rearranging
or in uncertain hand trying
to revive the brightness in them

librarians

(for Jan Horner)

come fall the libra
rians those libertarians
        are tremb
                        ling in the greatest deli
                ght handy with syll

able on waves of deli
quescence liable to go
                over the top
in bursts of delinquency

        enough deli
berations they are ruled
by the planet venus and
they have had enough of
schedules and budgets dream of
libido and apostasy of
flinging scarves & ties
list and definition
in gay libations loud celeb

                rations & ratios defi
                lers of deli
                cacy & celib
                acy co.
                                smonauts thrown by words
                                among the shelves & key
                                boards playing with dig

                              its its exciting to be
                         removing the dust jackets

        until having caught Hermes flat-footed
        and wakened by *vers libres* they
        leap tables hurdle computers
        in a hurricane release
        their squeezed voices spring
        from the archives sweep
        tumultuously from the stacks

        jump first thing feet-first
        into the unformed uninformed world
        ex nihilo, ex libris, ex
                              hilarating

the muse seeks the secrets of the universe

why this
is this
& not
that i can
not say
what you wish me to
do nor can i say
why this is
so   & so
i do & do

not now know no
nor care to
know i do not
know nor do i want to
carry rain in a knot
a knap
sack tied to
a sadsack & sunsick heart

knowing she did not pull
or tighten the strings she did not

leap into the wind upon her face
though you will have
spotted her dear reader

where she plunges into the dawn
pinching light from the planets
gathering secrets from plants

on to logical concerns

we have your name
you know we know

who you are
and why you are here

when when is now
we know what is what

and who is who
& what is more

what is up &
what (it) is to be

feeling down &
badly done-by

(un) done in
all you write

we also know
one is one

and two is some
times too

the muse calls

for a little

truth she says

she's fed up

with him, poet, rowing

wet-haired across the creeks & estuaries of life
encumbered with muddled thoughts

says first thing you beat it
and you never write
never a word of thanks

you have no shame you play
fast and loose with the facts
can never remember
what i whisper in the stirry dark,
and sometimes spinny day
you would lose if not pinned to your back:

**These words have I,
The Muse, provided.
if you find them,
Please return them
To the rightful owner.**

is it not enough i favour you
with gifts too intimate to tell
a lot of poets would die to receive

i hope they find you
languishing & short
        of breath
pining for your irretrievable losses

she tries to rally him

the sounds slide out of your arm
you and your ramshackle heart
nothing for a girl to lean or rely on
you who sashay and sidle

you should take it out
of your side, your heart i mean
idler amidst the newspapers and broken boxes
carry it solemnly in an empty soup can

do not throw it away
do not discard it
in a soupçon of despondency
a stray mutt i await
in snuffs & probings
have only fleas to offer

if you were now
and then to scratch my ear
i could cry out in an endearing
and passably soulful way

in the back yard of your weedy heart
i will dig my way in a fever
stop only to sniff and consider
the wart your life has become
to dwell in the smelly imbiss
of your rotten and impossible words

if you at all tried you could learn to care
for me on the splintered steps
the frozen slopes of january
when i leap clicking and
slobbery to the call

she still woos her muse

glamorous is not asking too much

                                    ¿ is it

that there would be more of us
more than a little for us & a little
something special for me

you could be a matinee
idol in cigarette flick
in the nick of time
idling through the lights

when you come & go
revolving through the black
doors slamming in your heart
a valentine full of thorns & roses
flashings of teeth & breath

            same goes for me
im no different
            i got

                        this thing for you

            i wish you yourself
        were on to me
i wouldn't mind one little bit

                not even if it was true
        and you had it coming

rodentia

she feeling shrewd
showed him he had
made a few mistakes
when he wooed would
tighten the wires to his heart
which under her mini
strations sounded alarmingly
like a broken banjo

she eschewed his overtures
gnawed the stem down to the stump
until he thrilled and shuddered

he rued the day
she fed on his heart
dined fastidiously on
the tidbits and morsels

and she broke out in small arias
trills of relish & satisfaction
hymns of sangfroid and frisson

smiled with her yellow-sharp teeth
made discreet chewy sounds
her small satisfied mouth

her nibbly kisses

rescue mission

talk about a terrible under
taking his heart turns black

in quixotic attempts
to bring her back
from the ravishing
dead she calls and
hearing he turns

        back peers down the steps
        into the dim hall

        from which
        they hope to flee

        it is not he says
        a man in white i see
        spiraling into the dark

        it is yr id
                IC

beat it, she said

he had been thinking
he should send her

a message in a bottle
brown seemed right
though she he knew
would prefer clear
a bottle she could peer through
from the other side of the ocean
see blue squid and lolly-legged octopi
him too, glued like a spider to the bottom

she would expect him
to adjourn the day and
shove it off into a distant sky
his letter in overture to a choppy wind
and it would make beautiful sounds
when she held it and blew on the lip

it would be he liked to think
an adventure a privi
ledge to be running poems
in a diplomatic pouch
all that contraband
the odd ship passing in the night
all day and not a gull in sight

it occurred to him sooner or later
there would be a handful of them
reformed sailors taking pot shots
a **SPLONNNK** and loud cheering when they hit

hoping to take it down
like a jar of spoiled preserves

under the streets

"This is the place I told you to expect."
—Dante, Inferno, Canto III (trans. John Ciardi)

Ω

the cold revolved in spokes
on which we wobbled
and shook like petunias

he himself was a musician he said
almost certainly a magician
his breath a small cloud of sleet
when he leaned over us
our glasses filmed and we turned
blue the table coated in frost

      he smiled like a urinal when he coughed
(the virtuous had nothing
              to fear (and he slammed the day
                like a cash register

          exits were strictly for
              bidden there would be
                  no way out
          we may as well give up
          all hope we who had entered here

his words slid in floes
and he blew loudly into
            a cold jar until
we were frozen shut
  in shouts & echoes

Ω
Lethal arrow shot
killed the Iceman

Scientists to
day said yes
terday they have
solved the 5,
000 year old my
stery of what
killed the ice
man, a Bronze
Age hunter whose fro
zen body was dis
covered a dec
ade ago in the
Alps: He was
shot by an ar
row near BOLZA
NO, Italy
.

Ω

the pale figures had arrived from rain
   from violins and easter chocolate and amber
        from the april square in Kraków
          where tulips in their cool thick flesh
turned yellow & red faces
      and tin pails held
    their palegreen arms
  against the chill

Ω

  the windows must have shaken
  the leaves rattled the snow
  whipped and stung it nearly
  sucked our breath away

Ω

Gostner said the path the arrow
followed as it ripped through his
body can be traced on the bones,
the ANSA news agency re-
ported. It appears the Iceman
could have lived only a few hours
after he was wounded.

Ω

Franklin on the Erebus and
Terror encrusted in the Arctic

Ω

the woman ate & drank
               nothing wore
her heart on her sleeve
blood-red as a pomegranate
filled to bursting she herself
white and breathless
and she raised her hand
the thin wan woman
on the edge of the ice fields
where she seemed to have wandered

excuse me
we wish to talk now

perhaps she contemplated throwing
her heart, lobbing it into the bunker
where the man railed

his voice cracked the stones
stiff for want of sun
we could hear them knocking
till they boomed like curling rocks

Ω

and we fled across slabs of ice

a grand larceny of hope
dogs yelping sleds bouncing
feared we would crash & spill our breath
in shredded banners behind us

the air rushing
                our faces burning
                        up the stone throat
                shivering &
                                coughing
                                        into the street
                Ω

His superbly pre served
corpse is kept in a
refrigerated   viewing
chamber at the South
Tyrol   Museum   of
Archaeology in Bolzano,
in northern Italy.

he foresees his end

he cannot forestall
not though the sun
which normally flips
like a tiddly wink plunges
with a gasp into the east
not though the winds quit their guzzling
or the stars in their quisling cease
to ferment and fizzle out like a fart

not though the fat-bellied moon itself
goes into a swoon and sinks
with a sloopy sound into the sea

or if at unexpected moments
they cry out like abandoned wallabies

      he will never
be over her it will never be
all over with her
                /never

              never
         the less dear reader
         you know he will lose
         his head will be left
         up the creek wailing
         among the algae and bald tires

you are not surprised
you know that
to say something

happened is happening
when we are touched & we come
into speech we are
in an old story

all the same
it is an old story
¿ isn't it

it tears me apart

thinking of you
it really does

tears you apart does it?

yeah i fall to pieces
when you are here
when you get near
when you are not here too

think that's bad wait'll i lay hands on you
we will rend you ear from ear and eat what's left
  /bone and all

you & your half-baked terracotta heart
your snot-nose snivellings
ill show you tearapart
you and your tearful two-bit songs
it'll be dearly departed it'll be
tears in the beer for you

ill show you terra incognita
ill show you a holy tearer
ill show you terribilità

he falls to pieces

                                    the enraged
Cicónian Bacchantes, in a nocturnal
Ritual orgy, tore his body to pieces
And scattered the pieces everywhere, far and wide
—Virgil's Georgics, trans. David Ferry

a busload of women laughing their heads off
and slapping their thighs like sumo wrestlers
they looked like head-hunters
headed his way they were
moving fast and rolling
their eyes like heifers in heat

he thought of pebbles falling into a well
into which words dropped like dust

their mouths were crowded with
every breath they took

they drew nearer he grew
light-headed his limbs began
to tingle   to feel numb
he grew sorely   afraid

                    he knew there was
                    nobody to pick up the pieces

                    no one to put him
                    back to gather again

terminal case

"Anything can happen now that we've slid over this bridge,"
I thought; "anything at all...."
     —Nick Carraway in The Great Gatsby

       ? where   she said
         ? where   ?is he

                where
    would she be
          on time
had she travelled light
entered the tunnels & gone

        missing the late muse
        had been delayed
        waylaid possibly
        memory unraveling

could be the cotton we wear near
our secret & imperishable hearts
    close to our sweet
and unspeakable thoughts

he wondered if she was out
of breath or time her hair stuck to her
forehead as she hurried one terminal to another

        she said she was
            coming he had to be
    going it was almost
                        time almost

        spring she was not
        to be seen he had
    to be going she was
    or was not coming

translations
(for Ela Leese)

i alone only i am
i only am escaped

*

i will see you
out he says when she says
she must be going

they are running out of time
all that time
breathing beneath the streets

*

the man with the lepral smile
the man so in love with himself
his words the only words

when he opens his mouth
crystals form in the air
a film of vapour over everything

what on earth were they thinking
where did they think
they were going

held himself in the vessel of his anger
until he was blue in the face
and they were too

*

       the sadness of her smile
              faint & fleeting

for a second she thought of absconding
her mouth wet and red with the fruit

         *

                she must have been
          smitten he thinks once bitten
            when you least suspect
sweet poison in the blood
and there is no going back

         *

       the white man shouted
        the windows shook

they winced when he spoke
his voice frozen sand against the glass

                  *

                in the end they
               had to breathe
             on their hands
              to keep them
             from freezing

*

listen she said

*
)he could have sworn
she limped
            /slightly
(alchemy of her words
her steps keeping time
        as she left(

music travelling like silk from her throat
when she turned into the corner of evening
breathing like a lighter
            moving like a scarf in may
            all the way home

IN ALL THINGS

for Diane

*"What after all is a poem
but a longing for a possible
reality?"*
—Robert Kroetsch, *The Hornbooks of Rita K*

visitation

when she leans
and speaks warmth
into his ear

he listens to the rainfall
of her speech he tries to
remember everything

he wants to carry away
hail stones in a bucket

all night his head aches
with the words he drags
in a leaking pail into morning

hopes to leave blue water
marks on the paper

dream letter

                              slip a paper
into an envelope of light
        under the door

        hoping for someone
                                        as if waiting
                                in the light
                waiting
        to hear

                in the morning
                                it is gone

something no one
can read and you
only dimly remember

1 East

              sky a wide broom
              whisks gray into blue
              a low rumble and boom

              sudden cold a
metallic click   then
                    duller
                      /harder

                      wet stones
                rattle across the roof
       across the blacktop

       pearls in a strange-half light
       burn when you hold them

the whack of cold
              turning to slush

       secretions around the specks of dust
       counting them out
           one by one
       the small tumults
       you thumb from the sun

you, waiting

                the seasons   swivel
                down   your neck

            months   circle their fences
             moths their   porch lights
            meant to   hold against
              owl   & weed

         the winds in their need   come & go &
              the years   lose their senses

         until you think of becoming   once more
             a bike buzzing   overhead risking all
          the loopy jeopardies   & licorice moustaches
          the malice chance sticks   in your spokes

      it doesn't matter   you pedal away pink
      knees pumping   as if your life depended

      on it you ride   down the spine time spins
      over   the adorations of spring
      beneath the aberrations of   saying
      you will   rise with skinned knees
      zip past slapping   ropes and chalked sidewalks

                off balance,   in love
                cheeks red   eyes shining

homecoming

a homesickness
   i have felt
      though i can
           hardly
              take
      a step
      barely make a
           sound

      you my muse
    and i your lazarus
sealed in encephalitis

      when you bend
    our bodies whizz and begin
   rolling into the streets

dream of you

                                    again

           you

on the other side

                                                once more

                there is a park   & you

a wide   open space &   you

                         way on the   other side

just before   the trees

                                                    silent and

                  palely waving

in tongues

blink of sun
the wind leaning
sky a tin rink
winter skated on

Montreal to Toronto
a memory of trains
          Mar 24 Via
Rail wet mitts
          their cake of winter
gramma cooley hangs
          on coalstove drips
through camphor drips the cold

on the back
          step, he stoops
where the afternoon hits
its shins & shines
          over the 25
                    gallon drum
its white skin
                    & he licks
          sticks tongue
tied to metal

)diane, young,
knelt tongue
    to rail   rail to tongue
          at Sioux Lookout

left a white tongue on the barrel
red tongue in the mouth

dear valentine

i am sorry to be   like this
writing you   two days late

only now   have i seen
what i am   to you

from   now on
you   can think

i am what   you sip
at your   rising

vagrance of your   attention

your hand
that close   that familiar

i have seen   you like this
when you talk   on the phone

the light falls   wetly
a yellow   you read & drink

something nearly   there
all   night long

something you   like
something   like this

reading

the brush of
your hand on the page

the book marks
the secret spot
you take and tuck
within the covers
and in faint hope open

your sun-dried thoughts
are turning to powder
alkali that rims a slough

dream the ink   will float
like pepper   to the surface

the yellowheads   on broken reeds calling
when they   settle back

she appears

                              you   me
        sea sick
                    star struck
your face a slow streak

            milk in coffee

fades in / fades out

your face is
    a planet turning

but then you speak

then when
is there

there is now
& there now will be

when ever we
see after

all that is
is all that

now we were
when then was now
& there was here

there it is
again when
it is new
when we are

not one then
this is when
this is after

just before
this then

in all things

i   take you with me

where   the two
            men sit   tweed suits
& then
            the table   empty
                a plate of sunlight

the   tablecloth   the glasses
shining   with the late afternoon
the empty room   or nearly

                smell of coffee &
        you there
            in the room
    sweet silence
                the sun
                        leans into

            warm   linen
    the cup   in my hands

time happens

φ

all this time
you know
your life
has been
happening
a teaspoon of light
every morning
a harpoon in your side
small tear in the flesh

φ

small tear in the flesh
a harpoon in your side
every morning
a teaspoon of light
happening
has been
your life
you know
all this time

radio at night

the boulder upon which
the world is splashing
its wishes swish ashore

when i row toward
your voice a radio
turned low at night

the large muscle
of your open heart
is lapping with the water's motion

the waves slosh softly against the dock
hopehope hopehope they say
                          your face
                          carried on the low tide
the slippery shape of tomorrow

AND YOU, DEAR READER

"What god was it, O Muses, Who devised / An art like this?"
—Virgil, *The Georgics of Virgil,* trans. David Ferry

apology

it may be   true.
it may be   time.
you may be   right.
i or you
      or both.

took everything
every thing
from the poet tree

a poem for you

YOUR POEM HE RE ·YOUR POEM HE
RE ·YOURP OEMHER E·Y OUR POEM
HERE ·YOUR POE M HERE ·
YOURPOEMH E RE· YOUR P
OEM H ERE · YOUR PO
E M HERE · YOURPOE
M HERE·Y OUR POE
M H E RE ·YOUR
POE M HE R E ·YO
URPOE MHE RE·YOU R PO E
M HE RE ·Y OUR POE M HERE ·Y
O UR P OEMHERE· YOUR POE
M H E RE ·YOUR POEM H
E R E ·YO URPOEMHERE·YOU
R PO EM HERE ·YOUR P
OE M HERE ·YOU
RP OE MHERE·YOU
R PO EM HERE ·YO U R
P O EM HERE ·YOURP OE
MH ERE·YOUR POEM HE RE ·YOUR
P OEM HER E ·YOURPOEMHER E·YOUR PO
E M HERE · YOUR POE M HERE ·
YOURPOE MHE RE·
YOUR P
OEM HE
RE ·YOU

The Muse Sings **Acknowledgments**

I am grateful to Matt Joudrey for inviting me into this project,
        and seeing it through,
and to Barbara Schott for her special care and insight.

Several of these pieces have appeared, in different versions,
in *Passwords, Soul Searching, Truck, F(e)asting Fitness, The
Society, Prairie Fire.*

The epigraph for "**COLLABORATIONS**" is from: Plato, *Ion.*
Apple Books.
https://books.apple.com/ca/book/ion/id498677805

The quotations in "Nefertiti" are from Wikipedia:
https://en.wikipedia.org/wiki/Nefertiti_Bust

The quotation, "A bracelet / of bright hair about the bone"
comes from John Donne's "The Relic"